Who Me? series co-editors: David A. Weintraub, Professor of Astronomy, of History, and of Communication of Science and Technology, College of Arts & Science, Vanderbilt University; Ann Neely, Professor Emerita of the Practice of Education, Peabody College of Education and Human Development, Vanderbilt University; and Kevin B. Johnson, David L. Cohen University Professor of Informatics, Engineering, Pediatrics, and Communication, University of Pennsylvania. Guest editors: Sammie Rosen and Geneva Bass.

Published by

WS Education, an imprint of

World Scientific Publishing Co. Pte. Ltd.

5 Toh Tuck Link, Singapore 596224

USA office: 27 Warren Street, Suite 401-402, Hackensack, NJ 07601

UK office: 57 Shelton Street, Covent Garden, London WC2H 9HE

British Library Cataloguing-in-Publication Data

A catalogue record for this book is available from the British Library.

Who Me? — Vol. 5

I'M A RADIATION ONCOLOGIST NOW!

978-981-127-301-8 (hardcover)
978-981-127-302-5 (ebook for institutions)
978-981-127-303-2 (ebook for individuals)

Desk Editor: Carmen Chan

Printed in Singapore

Image credits: Karen Winkfield: frontispiece, 4, 6, 7, 9, 10, 14, 16 bottom, 20, 21 top, 24, 32, 33, 35 top, 35 middle, 36, 37, 40 top, 41. **Shutterstock:** 11, 12, 13, 15, 16 top, 17, 18, 19, 21 bottom, 22, 23, 25 (eggs, pupa, moth), 27, 28, 29, 30, 34, 35 bottom, 38, 39, 40 bottom. **Goggy Davidowitz:** 25 (larval stages).

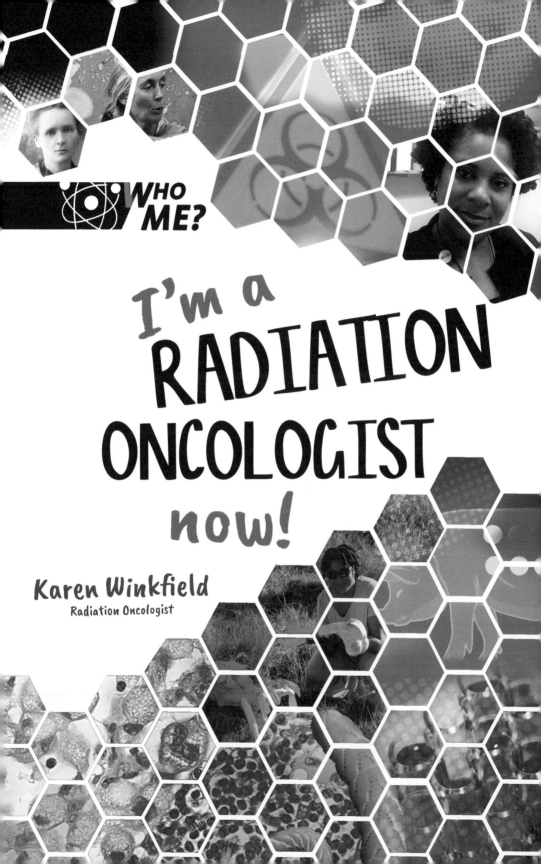

WHO ME?

I'm a
RADIATION
ONCOLOGIST
now!

Karen Winkfield
Radiation Oncologist

Table of contents

Hi! I am Karen Winkfield.

Karen in her lab, preparing to put on special glasses to study how proteins work.

Becoming Detective Winkfield

My name is Karen. I grew up in a small town in New York. I have six brothers and sisters, and I'm the youngest Winkfield. All of my brothers and sisters were talented. My talent was learning.

I practiced learning with my imagination. My favorite game was playing make-believe with my friends. My imagination made me curious. My curiosity turned the entire world into my classroom. I created worlds to escape to in my backyard or on the playground.

I loved reading. I especially liked to read science fiction and fantasy books. My all-time favorite book was *A Wrinkle in Time*. Reading this book made me wonder about things I did not understand. I even wondered about problems that nobody knew how to solve. I imagined how I would grow up and solve them! I also read all the *Nancy Drew* mystery stories. I always tried to solve these mysteries. I used my curiosity to act like Nancy Drew. I would solve mysteries every time I went outside. Before long, I wanted to grow up to become a detective.

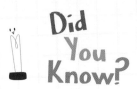

Did You Know?

Invent a Secret Code

Every good detective needs a method to send secrets to his or her team.

Use the symbols in this chart to decode this message:

♣^^@   ♥@%   ∞▲♥#∞

Letter	Symbol		Letter	Symbol
A	♥		N	@
B	Ω		O	^
C	◆		P	*
D	%		Q	ထ
E	!		R	#
F	4		S	∞
G	♠		T	▲
H	+		U	Π
I	©		V	∀
J	&		W	$
K	→		X	~
L	=		Y	]
M	♣		Z	9

Now, make your own chart. You can use your own symbols. For each letter of the alphabet, add a special character in the box next to that letter. Those special characters can be letters, numbers, symbols, or pictures. They will represent that letter in your secret code. You and your team of detectives can use your secret code to send messages to each other. You can even use your secret code to write stories!

When I first started going to school, I wasn't sure if I could trust my teachers. One day, during second grade, I was practicing my gymnastics with some friends during recess. I did a cartwheel and crashed into a fish tank. I cut my foot, but my teacher took care of me. She was so kind and concerned about me. I could tell how much she cared about me. After that experience, school became my happy place.

Karen's kindergarten class. Karen is in the middle row in the blue and white striped shirt.

In third grade, I learned about computers. I learned that computers use languages. In that way, computers are just like people.

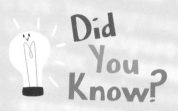

Did You Know?

What is a computer programming language?

Computers use languages to communicate, learn, and complete tasks. And just like in human languages, computer languages have rules about how different words can be combined. When these rules are followed, amazing things happen.

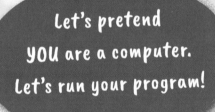

Let's pretend YOU are a computer. Let's run your program!

Your secret code uses symbols to represent information. Computers do that too. In this example, you will be a human computer. The symbols will be (A1), (A2), and (A3). Computer programmers call these symbols variables. That is because the values they represent can change.

In these three sentences, pick words to substitute for (A1), (A2), and (A3):

- The opposite of over is (A1).
- The opposite of never is (A2).
- If you take NO away from NOWHERE you get (A3).

Write them on a piece of paper:

(A1) =

(A2) =

(A3) =

Now be a computer and use the values you figured out for the variables.
Say this sentence the way a computer would: (A2) (A3) (A1) (A3)!!!
Now change (A2) to NEVER and run that program again!

That school year, I learned about the parts of the human body that are inside of us. I even held a human brain in my hands. I discovered that I liked learning about people and their lives. That is what detectives do. But being curious and learning about the human body is also what doctors do. Doctors solve real problems and help people.

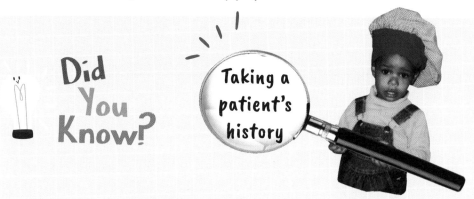
Imagine that you are a doctor. Pick a friend or someone in your family to be your patient. Ask them questions like these. They will help you learn about parts of their life that could be important to their medical care.

First, we need to find out a little about their **medical history**.

1. Has your patient ever broken a bone?
2. Has your patient ever gone to the emergency room or hospital due to illness?
3. Has your patient ever been hurt in a fight?

This medical history form indicates that the patient has asthma and diabetes.

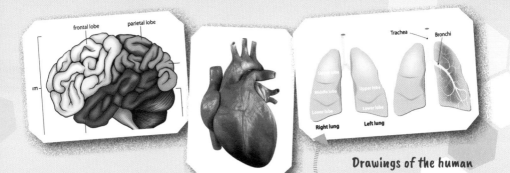

Drawings of the human brain, heart, and lungs.

Pick one of those questions and ask some more questions about your patient's history:

1. What happened?
2. When did it happen?
3. Why did it happen?
4. Did you go see a doctor? If so, what did he or she do?
5. How long did it take you to get over it?
6. Could you have prevented it?

Now, write up your patient's history. Other doctors who help your patient need to learn from the history you put together. Read it back to your patient. Was it correct? Show it to a friend. Did they understand everything you wrote?

A doctor and nurse reviewing a patient's medical history with the patient.

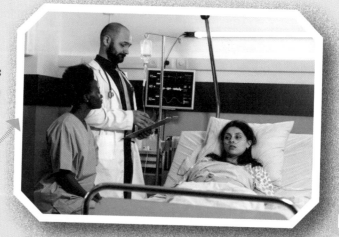

Fifth grade was a tough school year for me. My school closed and most of my friends went to a different school than me. I struggled without my friends. At the new school, I didn't fit in. Some of my classmates made fun of me for trying so hard in school. They teased me because I went to extra classes to learn more things.

I didn't like feeling like an outsider, so I stopped going to extra classes. I spent too much time worrying about what others thought. If I could go back in time, I wish I would have stayed in these classes so I could have continued to learn more interesting things.

I was in the Horticulture Club in middle school, where we learned about plants. I was also in the Science Club and on the math team. On top of that, I sang in the choir, played in the band, and ran for the track team. I had lots of energy and talked a lot. Once, I was kicked out of the Science Club for talking too much! I had to learn the right times for talking a lot.

Karen, with the microphone, singing to a group of younger children.

A saxophone, like the one I wanted to learn to play.

Music was important in my family. My father played the guitar and took us to concerts. We always played music on our camping vacations. We six kids would sing in harmony. I wanted to play the saxophone in a band. But saxophones cost a lot of money. My family could not afford to buy one. My school provided certain instruments to students whose families could not buy them. So I learned how to play the trombone instead.

A trombone, like the one I did learn to play.

I joined the middle school track team because I wanted to be on a sports team. Also, runners on the track team did not have to buy special clothes or equipment. In high school, the track coach told me I had to buy special running shoes called cleats. My family could not afford to do that. I was sad when I had to give up being on the track team just because my family had less money.

In high school, I was one of the only Black students in many of my classes. I had good teachers, but my first grade teacher, Mrs. Durant, was the only teacher I ever had before college who looked like me. I felt like an outsider, just like in fifth grade. But now I felt different because of the color of my skin. Still, I loved going to school and learning.

Working hard in high school and participating in clubs created opportunities for me and my future! At first, I did not understand that. Eventually, my teachers started asking me questions about my future. What did I want to do when I grew up? Did I want to go to college? My teachers thought I could go to college, even though I had never thought about doing that.

Karen's high school yearbook photo.

2 Homesick

Going to college was something new for my family.
Dad sold computers. Mom worked for the State of New
York. She stopped working when she became a mother.
None of my siblings went to college. But I wanted
to. My family did not understand why I wanted to
do something so different from what everyone else in
my family and community had done. My parents said
they would not pay to send me to college.

I needed to earn a **scholarship** to attend college. I
wanted to study music and become a singer. I applied
to four colleges. I had to sing in front of teachers
from each college. This is called an audition. It was
like being on *American Idol*, except the prize was a
college scholarship.

ACCEPTED!

After each audition, the teachers would decide if I was good enough of a singer to attend their college. The auditions made me nervous. I was scared. I worried that I would perform poorly. But I did well. The State University of New York at Binghamton offered me a full scholarship. This meant I was able to go to college for free!

When I started college, I was overwhelmed. Most of my classes were about singing and music. I loved my classes, but it seemed like everyone around me had a head start. Because I was the first of my siblings to go to college, I did not know what to do. I thought all my classmates came from families that knew about colleges. I thought they all knew what to do all the time. I felt like the only college student who didn't know what she was doing. I know now that lots of my classmates were worried and felt alone, just like me. But I didn't know that then.

I had never been away from home before. I missed my family. I was learning about things that were new to me. That was challenging. In some of my classes, I did not always have the right answers at my fingertips. That had never happened to me before. I began to think that I was not smart enough for college. I felt like I was wearing a backpack full of rocks. And a new rock was added to my backpack every day. I started to feel weighed down. I was sad, and I felt lonely. I didn't smile much. Sometimes, I was afraid. I had never experienced loneliness when living at home.

Eventually, my invisible backpack became too heavy for me to carry. I needed a break from college. After my second year, I took some time off. I needed to find my smile again. In my imagination, I took a break from college to search for my smile.

I moved to another city. I got a job in Washington, D.C., working in an office with lots of lawyers. I learned about the things that lawyers do. The lawyers enjoyed the work they did, but the things these lawyers did were not interesting to me. I learned that I did not want to be a lawyer. This discovery was important. Learning what I did not want to do helped me discover what I did want to do.

I did enjoy one part of my job. I was sent on business trips all over the world. Traveling opened my eyes to different ways of living. I decided I wanted a career that would give me the freedom to travel and learn even more about other parts of the world.

Karen while traveling in Botswana.

After a few years of traveling and working for the law firm, I became a mother. My daughter's name is Ashley. Being a mother to Ashley forced me to think about what type of role model I wanted to be for her. I decided to give music one more chance. I wanted to be able to tell her that I tried my hardest to become a singer. I moved to New York City with my baby to try to become a star. At the same time, I was also raising a baby on my own. This was too much for me to handle. But I look back on that time with no regrets. I know I did my best.

Karen with baby Ashley.

Karen hoped to perform in shows like these, in New York City.

Now I had to decide what to do next. I thought about the two things I loved most: singing and the science of the human body. I decided they were related to each other in a special way. Musical instruments produce sound waves. Our voice box is a musical instrument. It produces sound waves when we sing. Sound waves are a part of the science called physics. Sound waves travel through the air. We need special tools to notice sound waves passing by. Our ears can do that. Our ears detect those sound waves. Our ears then send information about the sound waves to our brains. We need our brains to understand the information collected by our ears.

Sound Waves

If you have been to the beach, you have seen waves coming toward the shore.

If you've wiggled a slinky toy, you've made waves.

An ocean wave.

Waves carry energy from one place to another. A big wave at the shore might have enough energy to knock you over. The energy in the wave moves when one object pushes the object next to it. In a water wave, one drop of water pushes the next one. Then, that drop of water pushes the next one. That is how a water wave travels across the ocean, a swimming pool, or a bathtub.

A person making a wave with a slinky.

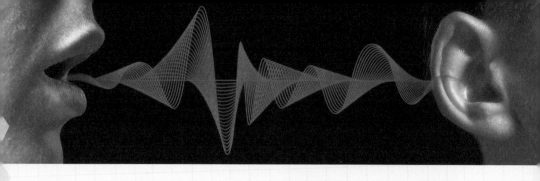

Sound waves travel through the air and are detected by us with our ears. When we speak, our muscles make our vocal cords wiggle. We call that wiggle a vibration. The wiggling vocal cords push on the air in our throats. The air in our throats pushes on the air in the room. In that way, a sound wave is pushed through the air.

When the sound wave is pushed into our ear, the air pushes on the part of our outer ear called the eardrum. The energy in the sound wave makes the eardrum vibrate. The vibrating eardrum makes some little bones in the middle ear vibrate. The little bones are called ossicles. These little bones push the fluid in our inner ear and make that fluid move. The moving fluid converts the wave into signals that are carried to our brains by nerves. What we call *hearing* is our brain's response to these signals.

When a sound wave is detected by the ear, information about that sound wave is sent to the brain.

Ashley, at age 3,
learning to be a puppeteer.

Ashley in her
kindergarten class.

Ears and brains are part of the science called biology. So I decided to return to college to become a scientist.

During my time away from college, I discovered that I loved science. I also had become a mother to Ashley. As a result, I was a very serious student. My college classes were not always easy. But I learned how to study and was a good student.

Two more things were incredibly important in helping me become successful in college. My college had a daycare center. I could bring Ashley there when I was in class. And my friends would take care of her when I needed help. I learned that my success depended on the kindness and support of others. My invisible backpack got lighter and lighter every day until it disappeared. I made a promise to myself. Someday I would find ways to help others. That is how I would repay the help I received.

My favorite classes were the science labs. In those labs, I learned how to be a scientist. I worked in a lab where we studied the tobacco hornworm. My task was to study how they create the shells of their cocoons.

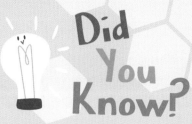

Life Cycle of the Tobacco Hornworm

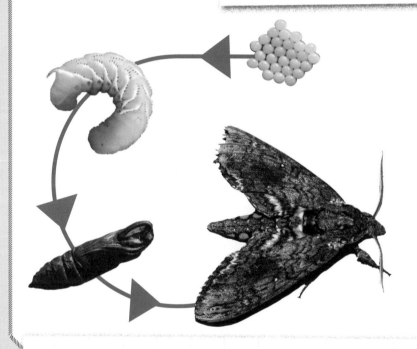

The tobacco hornworm begins its life as an egg. The eggs are laid on the undersides of leaves. When an egg hatches, it is called a larva. A larva is like a worm or a caterpillar. The larva grows for about 18 days. Most of the growth happens during the last few days. The larva then builds a cocoon around itself and becomes a pupa. The hornworm sleeps and grows inside its cocoon. When it creates the cocoon, it is a squirmy caterpillar. When it emerges from the cocoon, it has become a moth called a Carolina Sphinx Moth. It has gone through a process called **metamorphosis**.

Every day, going to the lab, I passed a sign. It hung on the door to the lab next to the name of the lab director. It read MD/PhD.

MD is the title given to a person who is a medical doctor. PhD is the title given to someone who is a scientist and does research. That's when I decided I wanted to be both a doctor and a scientist. To do that, I needed to graduate from college. Then, I needed to go to another school to learn even more.

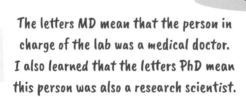

The letters MD mean that the person in charge of the lab was a medical doctor. I also learned that the letters PhD mean this person was also a research scientist.

3 Helping People Who Look Like Me

Ashley and I moved again. This time, we moved to North Carolina. That is where I studied to become a doctor and a scientist. I did not know yet what kind of doctor I wanted to become. But I knew I had to choose a specialty.

Different Kinds of Doctors

A pediatrician listening to a young child's heartbeat.

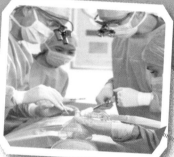

A group of surgeons working in an operating room.

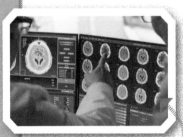

A radiologist studying images of a human brain.

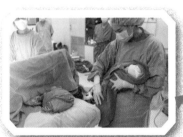

An obstetrician who has just delivered a baby.

A pathologist studying tissue samples with a microscope.

A dermatologist studying the skin of a patient.

In medical school, I worked in a research lab again. I studied the genes that can cause breast cancer. Breast cancer is the most common cancer in the world. This means that anything scientists learn about breast cancer could save a lot of lives.

Breast Cancer

AWARENESS MONTH

All living things are made of cells. Our bodies are made of skin cells, muscle cells, blood cells, brain cells, and lots of other kinds of cells. Inside each cell are genes. Genes are like the instruction manuals for toys you have to put together.

Human blood cells seen with a microscope.

If the instructions are written well, the toy will be built correctly and will work well. If the instructions are full of errors, the toys won't work properly. In all living things, genes control how each cell works. Genes tell a cell to be a skin cell, a heart cell, a blood cell, or a brain cell. Genes even provide instructions for telling each cell how to help heal our bodies. Healthy bodies need to make new cells to grow new skin, heal broken bones, and make fresh blood. Cells in healthy people reproduce when the body tells them to do so. One cell reproduces by dividing into two cells. And in healthy people, cells take one day to divide.

Cancer happens when a gene starts giving the wrong instructions. Genes in cancer cells instruct the cells to divide too often. The genes then instruct the cells to repeat that process over and over again. In most people, this does not happen. When cells divide too fast, the extra cells can make a bump. These bumps are called tumors. Doctors spot cancer cells by finding these tumors.

In the lab, I studied two different genes that cause breast cancer. One is called BRCA1. The other is called BRCA2. I started my research with an important clue. I knew that Black women are more likely to get hurt from breast cancer than white women. I wanted to know why. Detective Karen was on the job! If I could figure this out, I would be solving a scientific mystery. I would also be saving lives!

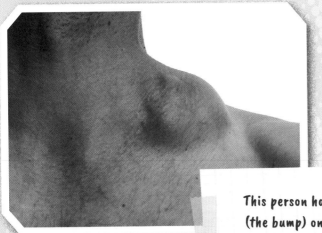

This person has a tumor (the bump) on his neck.

As a scientist, I needed a big question to try to answer. This is my big question. Are the instructions coded into these two genes different in Black women and white women?

Genes are parts of even larger sets of instructions for cells. Genes are parts of something called a DNA molecule. DNA molecules are found in every human cell. The DNA molecules in every cell in your body are identical. And they are unique to you. In fact, every person has their own, unique DNA molecule. Your DNA is like your fingerprints. Both your DNA and your fingerprints are different from those of every other person on Earth.

I needed to look at DNA molecules from both Black women and white women. For my research, I would search for differences. Scientists study DNA in blood samples. Those samples come from people who have donated blood samples to hospitals. But I had a problem. I could not do my research project because very few Black women had donated their blood samples. I wondered why. Detective Karen had another mystery to solve!

A nurse wearing a protective suit is taking a blood sample from a female patient.

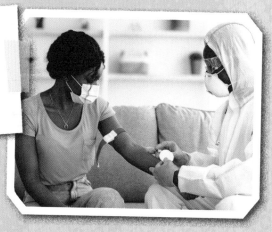

Different DNA?

I asked more questions. I wanted to learn about experiments called clinical trials. In clinical trials, doctors test new medicines on volunteers. This is how scientists learn if new medicines work.

I learned that few Black people enroll in clinical trials. That is a problem. Without Black people in their studies, doctors cannot learn whether a new medicine will help them in the same way. I had detected a pattern. Even when Black people were treated as patients at the hospital, many did not participate in research. I did not understand why.

I learned that not everyone can get healthcare. Some people cannot afford to pay doctors. And sometimes hospitals are hard to find in the parts of cities where they live. And some people do not trust their doctors. Perhaps they or someone they know received poor treatment in the past. Or maybe they would feel better having a doctor who looks like them. All these things could be reasons why fewer Black people choose to be involved in medical research.

I talked about this problem with my teachers. That was when I discovered that very few doctors at my hospital were Black. In fact, there are very few doctors who look like me in the whole country!

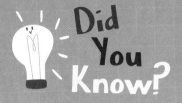

Did You Know?

Meharry Medical College

Today, I work at both Meharry Medical College and Vanderbilt University Medical Center in Nashville, Tennessee. Meharry was founded in 1876. It was the first medical school in the American South that allowed Black people to train to become doctors. For more than 100 years, it was one of the only medical schools in the United States that trained Black people for careers in medicine. Today, Meharry still trains students to become doctors, dentists, research scientists, and health policy experts.

I now help young Black people who want to become doctors and nurses. I also help get more Black people to participate in medical research.

Did You Know?

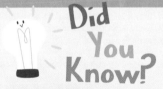

Teaching others about healthcare careers

I direct the Meharry-Vanderbilt Alliance. I teach people about healthcare. Sometimes I go to big fairs to teach people. I can also teach people by speaking on the radio or TV.

I also help young people learn about careers in medicine. They might become doctors or nurses. Or they might become medical technicians and physical therapists.

I work with youths in middle schools and high schools. I work with students in college and medical school. I also train young doctors and scientists. I love helping them succeed.

Karen, on the *Dr. Lonnie Joe* television show, talking about healthcare issues that affect Black people.

Karen, on a radio show, answering questions about healthcare.

4 Making Treatment Better for Everyone

One of the specialties I learned about in medical school is called oncology. Oncologists work with patients who have cancer. I had lots of experience working with cancer cells. But I had no experience helping people who have cancer. Soon, that changed.

I met a patient who changed my life. She helped me realize that cancer is more than cells in a dish in my lab. I saw how scared she was in the hospital. I decided that I would spend part of every workday in the lab being a scientist. Then I would spend the remaining part of every workday being a doctor and helping patients.

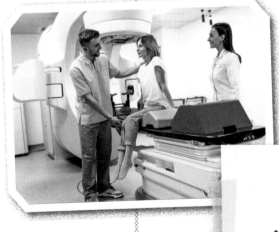

An oncologist and a medical technician preparing a patient for cancer treatment.

When it was time for me to pick a specialty, I decided to become an oncologist. I would use X-rays to help patients. To become a radiation oncologist, I needed special training at a different hospital. So, after medical school, I moved again. This time I moved to Boston.

Living in Boston was a fun time for me. I even sang the national anthem at a Boston Red Sox baseball game at Fenway Park!

Karen in her office in Boston.

Radiation is one way of helping people with cancer. Radiation is the word scientists use for energy traveling through space. The light our eyes can see is one kind of radiation. X-rays are another kind of radiation. It is a kind of light your eyes cannot see. X-rays can go all the way through our bodies, but not through our bones. If you break a bone, doctors use a very weak beam of X-rays to look inside your body and see where your bone is broken. They use that information to decide how to help heal your broken bone.

That's me, up on the big screen at Fenway Park, singing the national anthem for 37 thousand fans, plus more watching on television!

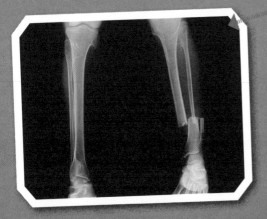

An X-ray image of a person with one healthy leg (left) and one broken leg (right). X-rays go right through skin and muscle, but are stopped by bones. So with X-rays, doctors can take pictures of the bones to find where a bone is broken.

Radiation oncologists use powerful beams of X-rays to treat cancer. By aiming those beams of X-rays at tumors, doctors can kill cancer cells. With X-rays, doctors can destroy tumors without doing surgery. That's the good news. The bad news? X-rays can also damage healthy tissues in our bodies. The damage to healthy tissue is called a side effect of cancer treatment.

I want to learn how to treat cancer without causing side effects. One common side effect of exposure to X-rays is skin damage. Skin damage can happen at places where X-rays go through the skin. When we used X-rays on white patients, their skin would sometimes turn red or start peeling. Doctors use medicines to stop this painful process!

The picture shows a patch of skin of a patient that has become darker after X-ray treatments. The darkening occurs just before the skin blisters. A red blister is seen on the left side of the picture.

However, for Black patients with darker skin, their skin did not always get red and would sometimes peel more. Detective Karen was back in action! Does darker skin respond to X-rays in different ways than lighter skin? Or do doctors just have a hard time seeing the injured skin? Nobody knew how to answer these questions.

I wanted to find out how different skin colors react to X-ray treatments. I knew my research could help other doctors help their patients.

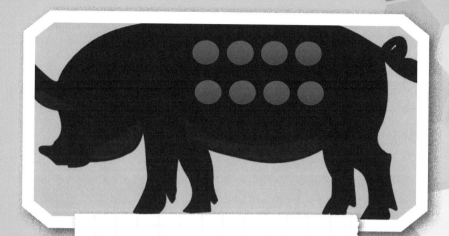

We exposed circular patches on the skin of a pig to X-rays. Before using the X-rays, the circular patches were coated with different amounts of a special cream or with salt water.

I decided to find a better way to describe the changes seen in darker skin. A big change could mean the patient needs special care to ensure their skin does not get damaged. But doctors did not have a good way to measure changes in patients with darker skin color.

I decided to do an experiment. I found pigs with light skin and others with dark skin. Then I measured how their skin changed after radiation. The experiment was successful. We learned that lighter skin turns red and then peels. We also learned that darker skin does not turn red. Instead, it becomes even darker. Doctors call this kind of change in skin color **hyperpigmentation**.

Did You Know?

What is pigmentation?

Pigmentation has nothing to do with pigs!

Pigments are the materials that make other materials dark or light or blue or red. A paint store worker could put drops of special pigments into white paint to change the color to the one a painter wanted to use.

Pigmentation refers to the coloring of skin. Some people have light-colored skin. Others have dark-colored skin. Some people with light skin can have dark skin spots, and some people with dark skin can have light spots. Skin color can even change when exposed to sunlight. The pigment that gives color to human skin color is called melanin.

Adding black pigment to white paint to make black paint.

Paints of different colors.

FITZPATRICK SCALE

DARK BROWN   BROWN   OLIVE   MEDIUM   FAIR   VERY FAIR

This chart helps doctors predict a person's risk of being tanned or burned by sunlight. Which skin colors have more pigment? Which skin colors are more likely to get burned by sunlight?

We invented a scale to help researchers describe the side effect that different amounts of X-rays have on darker skin. This tool is called the Winkfield Hyperpigmentation Scale. It works for pigs! We can use this scale to predict how pig skin will react in response to the radiation.

Next, we have to use this knowledge about pig skin to learn about human skin. Someday, this new knowledge will help doctors. They will be able to better predict when a patient with darker skin is having a side effect from X-rays. Doctors can then design a special combination of skin care or medicine for each patient. Patients will suffer less skin damage. Scars on their skin will not form as often. They will have less pain from side effects.

If I could go back in time, I would change nothing.

If I could go back in time, I would change nothing. I followed a path that led me to the work I do now. All of the things I learned while I was making discoveries about what I liked and what I wanted to do helped me today.

When I was 10 years old, I did not know that I would become a doctor and scientist. Even at age 20, I had not yet discovered what I wanted to do for my career. You don't always know what you are doing and why. I am grateful for my journey.

I tell the students I work with to be open to new experiences. I think all of the experiences I had on the path I took had value. I also tell them to accept that some doors may be closed to them. Closed doors can lead us to other opportunities.

Some doors will be open while others may be closed.

Talking to young people is one way I return the favors of the many people who helped me become a doctor and scientist.

My advice to you is to just be yourself. Believe in yourself and do not allow doubt to creep in. There are many pressures on all of us. Some may come from your family. Some may come from teachers or friends. Lots of people told me I was not going to succeed in college or medical school. I was taking care of my daughter, Ashley, alone. I had to work hard.

I sometimes had to ask others for help. Asking for help was a sign of strength! I had to have the help and support of others. And I succeeded! Now, I am returning the favors so many others did for me. So, who am I? I am a doctor and a scientist. And I am a detective!

GLOSSARY

Clinical Trial

An experiment in which doctors test new medicines or medical procedures on people who volunteer to be part of the experiment.

Genes

A part of every cell in your body that tells it how to work. Your hair color and eye color are determined by your genes.

Hyperpigmentation

A change in skin color in which dark skin becomes even darker.

Medical history

Information about a person's health, including allergies, surgeries, illnesses, immunizations, and injuries.

Melanin

A pigment found in hair, skin, and eyes of animals and people that controls color.

Metamorphosis

A process through which the body structure of an animal transforms from one shape to another.

Oncology

The study of cancer.

Ossicles	Tiny bones in our ears. They are the tiniest bones in the human body.
Pigments	Materials that give other materials their color.
Proteins	Molecules in our bodies that make up structures in our body and carry out the chemical reactions that keep us alive.
Radiation	Energy transported through space. Radiation can be in the form of light or particles.
Radiation Oncologist	A medical doctor who uses X-rays to treat patients who have cancer.
Scholarship	Money given by a college or foundation to a student to help pay the costs of their education.
Side effect	Something that happens as a result of taking medicine or undergoing medical treatment that is not intended.

Discussion Questions

1. Can you think of ways or reasons why some people might receive better healthcare than others?

2. Why might a person seek out help from a dermatologist? An allergist? An orthopedist? A pediatrician?

3. Do you know anyone who has worn a pink ribbon for cancer awareness month? Why do you think they did that?

4. In the experiment Dr. Winkfield did with pig skin, why do you think some skin spots were covered with a special cream but others were covered with salt water?

Additional Resources

1. Meharry-Vanderbilt Alliance:

2. What is cancer?:

3. National Breast Cancer Awareness Month (in the United States):

4. National Cancer Prevention Month:

5. Medical specialists who work with children: